HOJOJUTSU

The Binding Art   Vol. 1

By Shihan Allen Woodman

SIDEKICK Publications 2014

ISBN-13: 978-1495935206
ISBN-10: 1495935205

Hojōjutsu The Binding Art Volume 1 Written by Shihan Allen Woodman
SIDEKICK PUBLICATIONS, Allen Woodman 1st printing Copyright – 2014 Printed in U.S.A. 2014

Dedicated

To the teachers of my past. May you all find peace and
comfort in the legacy I continue in your name.

My Deepest respects to you all!

~Shihan Allen Woodman

Table of Contents

Forward By Shihan Dana Abbott 6

Preface By Allen Woodman.. 10

Chapter Two – Understanding the Art 14

Chapter Two – Bind Us in Unity.................................... 28

Chapter Three – Techniques / Rear Attack 1 34

Chapter Four – Rear Attack #2.................................... 42

Chapter Five – Front Attack Punch #1 52

Chapter Six – Front Attack Punch #2............................ 66

Chapter Seven – Front Punch Attack #3......................... 76

Chapter Eight – Front Kick Defense #1 86

Chapter Nine – Double Punch Defense #1 100

Chapter Ten – Revise Old for New................................ 114

Chapter Eleven – About the Author.............................. 120

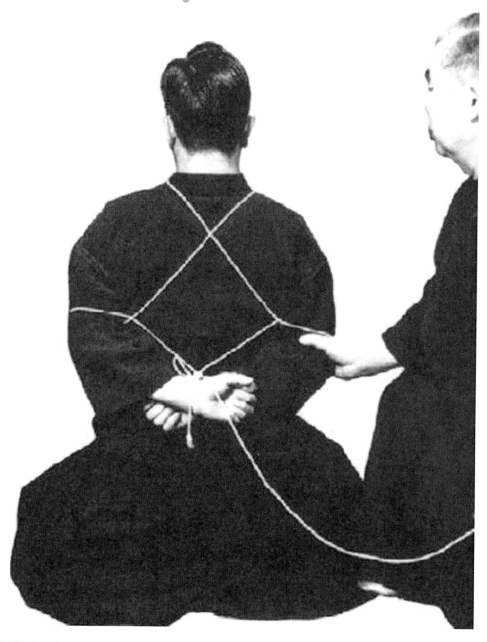

Forward

Shihan Dana Abbott

When Shihan Allen Woodman asked me to write a foreword for this book I was first hesitant to do so. I was not an authority on the art of Hojojutsu but I have used it. After some contemplation I wrote what I thought would be an honest example of the art as I know it to be.

What is Hojojutsu and what is its origin and purpose. Shihan Allen Woodman's book will answer all those questions. To put Hojojutsu into a perspective and mental image that you can better comprehend ...imagine this...

In the foothills of Mt Fuji is where the time honored "Drum Festival" takes place. This is a yearly function attended by only the very best drummers chosen from every village in Japan. It was their aim to take home the sought after prize which was a great honor.

All morning long spectators had been arriving, some on horseback and others on foot. By midday, half of the entrants had performed and it was obvious some of these groups would be difficult to beat.

My fellow samurai and I had been observing the area watching the crowds. Most were enjoying the festivities of the day but there was a group of malcontents that were displeased that their village group had not placed higher in the competition and their agitation was rising to a feverish point.

As a new band rose to perform a few of the drunken malcontents became violent and started to shove over some of the drums. Enough is enough ran through

my head. I grabbed one of them by the wrist and yanked him around. To my astonishment he pulled out a short slender bladed knife from underneath his obi and attempted to slash me. I immediately grabbed the offending limb forcing him to the ground and snapping his arm in two places.

As he screamed in pain I grabbed my coiled rope from my hip easily threading it around his broken arm, across his back and pinning it against his other arm which bound them together. I arrested him on the spot using the weight of my knee on his back to hold him down. His knife, now lying several feet away, is picked up by another who then also lunges toward me in a threatening manner.

While my free hand holds the tail end of the rope, I automatically reach upward snaring the second attacker's hand thus intercepting and deflecting his blade. I yank downwards seeing the blade drop followed by him tumbling after it. In his mid-air flight I again yank and redirected his hand which landed him on top of his friend. I swiftly but methodically, bind his hands together while throwing a loop around his neck and securing it just tight enough so as not to choke him...unless the other guy moves.

Now that you have some insight on how Hojojutsu has been traditionally used in everyday life by the samurai you can further your enjoyment of Shihan Woodman's book.

About Shihan Dana Abbott

Dana Gregory Abbott for 35 years has been training in the Art of the Samurai and the Way of the Sword. For over 15 years he trained, studied, and lived in Japan, practicing under the direction of some Japan's most respected teachers.

Shihan Dana Abbott's bladed weaponry experience is extensive, focused and well-polished. He has taught and conducted seminars in over 30 countries. He is honored to hold the esteemed rank of Shihan 7th Dan, in the sword art of

Goshindo, obtained at the Hombu Dojo in Yokohama, Japan.

The following awards have been bestowed upon Dana Gregory Abbott Shihan:

- *Black Belt* Magazine Hall of Fame, Weapons Instructor of the year 2004

- United States Martial Arts Hall of Fame

- Universal Martial Arts Halls of Fame

- *Action Martial Arts* Magazine Hall of Fame

- World Karate Union Hall of Fame

- Masters Hall of Fame

Shihan Shihan Abbott in his own easily taught method is able to instruct in a clear, concise, Zen-like fashion geared for both beginner and experienced alike. This has proved to be quite successful for him instructing the "spirit of the thing" throughout the United States.

For any questions or for more information please contact

Shihan Dana Abbott at

Samurai Sports
31211 N. 64th Street
Cave Creek, AZ
85331

480-575-7319

Preface

By Allen Woodman

Hello and thank you for reading the newest addition in the Defensive Hojojutsu system that I teach.

In this manual you will find many techniques using the intricate and delicate art of Hojojutsu: the Art of Binding. This book and the material found inside is in itself a new approach to self-defense with a very traditional taste of old word Japanese style and custom.

The art and style that I teach is not the classical Japanese art of Hojojutsu as it has been seen or taught through other sources. The system that I teach is an integrated and compendium of several schools of training and teaching. The techniques that will be seen in this collection are the techniques that I teach around the world in informative lectures and seminars with hands on experience. These techniques are invaluable and reflect my personal approach to defense using the rope, cord or belt.

The main approach that I have taken in developing the techniques of the Hojojutsu system is a quick catch or defensive movement that will ultimately end in the sublimation of an opponent or attacker. The techniques taught herein reflect my attention to allow a person to defend quickly and subdue their opponent in a variety of different approaches and scenarios. From defenses applied from the rear or in a full frontal attack these techniques have been proven to be not only effective but easy to apply as well.

In my forty years plus involved in martial arts I honestly feel that the art of Hojojutsu is a well-rounded system that can be applied by the defender swiftly and safely.

In today's world of fast action and the ever growing mixed martial arts or MMA industry, I feel that it is important to look back at the more traditional roots of martial arts. The foundations of the arts that gave us todays leading schools and practices. These foundations are the true building blocks of martial arts and more so Hojojutsu are the richest elements of true battle tested techniques that have been passed down from teacher to student for more than 500 years of recorded history.

The basics of Hojojutsu and those of my own predecessors are grounded in the same viable arts and teachings that have gone relatively unchanged for as many years. There is a reason that those techniques have not changed or been redressed for the sake of changing times. The body itself has not changed in more than one hundred thousand years or more. In that time the development of martial arts and self-defense. We as humans have two arms and two legs with a torso in between. The body turns, rotates, moves and undulates on several points of balance and stability. Therefore the body only moves in a select few ways. Learning the body and the effects that it carries in movement has been a lifelong search for martial artist. Through the practice and study of martial arts and its intricacies the defender can address an attacker on an even balance scale.

The study of Hojojutsu is the development of an external extension of the body. This extension is developed by way of the rope or cord used. The cord, rope, belt or other elongated braid of cloth can not only add extension to the length of defense and range but adds power and stability as well.

Within the system of Hojojutsu as I can explain it, the use of such fabric or ropes can increase the strength and power of its user 3 x greater in application. This greatly adds a benefit to Hojojutsu usage. The extra strength and holding power allows a person to subdue and restrain an attacker from various scenarios. Using the cord or rope quickly defends position in an altercation or allows for an unexpected defensive movement that can easily overtake an opponent with trained skill and reserve.

With any martial art, it does take a measured and trained skill that is developed over time. Nothing can be learned in a minute of viewing. It is like any other martial art or ability. It must be trained and honed to be useful and productive.

Please take the material found in this manual with the care and safety that it requires and remember to practice slowly, safely and securely.

All my best in Budo

~Allen Woodman

Chapter 1

Understanding the Art

Hojojutsu is the beautiful and peculiar art of restraining someone using (often brightly colored) cord. It is rarely practiced outside of Japan and is an ancient strand of martial art with a rich and complex history. Hojojutsu is seldom taught as an isolated art form, it usually constitutes a single aspect in the study of a much wider curriculum as advanced jujutsu. The art of binding objects is traditionally Japanese, whether it be tying on kimonos or even finishing wrapped gifts with decorative cord and elaborate knot work or the more simple method of transporting objects, luggage and foodstuffs in fabric secured with cord or rope, we know that the habit of tying up objects runs deeply through Japanese culture.

The use of rope or cord on the battlefield is most often thought of in terms of lanyards or simply as coils of rope for use in tying, climbing, etc.

Yet, to varying degrees in in different parts of the world, rope or cord has seen use as a primary weapon.

In Europe, some medieval fighting masters recognized that rope had a use in defensive combat.

15th century fighting Master Fiore Dei Liberi ca. 1340s – 1420s) was a late 14th Century knight, diplomat, and itinerant fencing master. He is the earliest Italian master who wrote one of the foremost literary martial arts manuals. His Flor Di Battaglia or *Flower of Battle* is the third-oldest European fencing manual discovered as well as being the most

extensive from the medieval period. In his manual, Fiore mentions that the rope can be used in defense even against a dagger or small staff.

In Asia the use of cord or rope as a weapon is ancient, and has been historically documented. Usually classed as part of "unarmed combat", rope has been seen as a primary weapon in the combat arts of India the Philippines and China, where a variety of rope-based weapons and combat techniques are gathered under the heading of "soft weapons", and indeed, was used by

Chinese police as late as the 1920's where a manual on the use of rope in arresting criminals was issued by the Shanghai Police Training Center (Rope Capture Techniques for Arrest/Detainment). In almost all cases, the rope is used as much to trip, entangle and restrain enemies as it is for causing injury.

The use of the rope in combat reached a high art in Japan, where the cord which tied the katana to a warrior's belt (the sageo) also was used to tie up the sleeves of the warrior's kimono, and if a prisoner was captured could then be removed and used to tie captured samurai. This art of tying prisoners became its own, separate art, Hojojutsu.

As time passed, this art became a tool of civilian police as well as a battlefield skill, becoming part of the police officer's martial art repertoire later known as Taihojutsu. Techniques were developed using small coils of rope called "Nawa", which allowed police to block and parry armed attacks, simultaneously snagging the wrists or arms of law-breakers.

The art form known a Hojojutsu is a study of more than just the immediate fast-tying of an opponent. It also included the art of knot tying or musubi. According to many masters of Hojojutsu, there were four main rules of the art:

1. Not to allow the prisoner to slip his bonds.
2. Not to cause any physical or mental injury.
3. Not to allow others to see the techniques.
4. To make the result beautiful to look at.

Number three above is listed because, of course, the techniques and knot-work had to be kept secret in order that criminals wouldn't learn to counter them. Number four is a cultural note; in Japanese society, everything had to have an esthetic side. Important prisoners (from samurai families for example), could not simply be roughly tied, but must be tied in a manner pleasing to the eye. In fact, for prisoners of this class there were specific "wrapping" techniques developed which bound the prisoner but used no knots at all. Being arrested at all was shameful, but being transported with knotted ropes indicated the person was guilty of a crime, and as such knotted bindings were considered very dishonorable.

Any official Torimono (police officer trained to apprehend prisoners) was expected to be able to restrain and tie their prisoner within ten seconds or less. According to historians and martial arts experts, at its height of use, there were over 150 separate schools of Hojojutsu in Japan, each with its own secret techniques.

Techniques from one school of training were never traded or taught to other schools of training. These skills would never be allowed to be seen by other schools or students of other schools as to protect their secret binding techniques and musubi knots. The various ties and knots always vary and differ from one school to another. Although similarities may be present, the overall approach and final musubi tie would never be the same as a different school of learning.

The reason for this is very simplistic, due to the feudal periods in which they blossomed there was never a settled or secure period in which one prefecture was not at war or in a position of war with another neighboring prefecture. Therefore the students of such schools would never want a potential enemy or threat to know the intricate details of their style of submission because they may possibly be tied up in the future with those techniques. Thus avoiding possible attempts of escape by detainees.

The main purpose of maintaining secrecy was so that captives did not learn ways to escape the bonds. This rule was kept so diligently that often if a prisoner was being escorted across the country, most restraining knots would be loosened as they approached the destination to prevent the other domain's officers from learning techniques used in a different domain.

Although the precise origins of this art form are unclear, the reason behind the process is pretty evident. Hostages and prisoners were secured in this manner during transportation. The advanced nature of this practice differed greatly with what was occurring throughout the rest of the world where there were much simpler devices used for restraining prisoners such as metal (smithed) cuffs or leather bindings.

The Art of Hojojutsu is not in itself a system or complete art. It is a subsection or a compartment to other traditional schools of learning with in the traditional Japanese Jujutsu Do or Way of learning. Within these pages are techniques that I have learned and developed through years of training and practice from various schools of Jujutsu. These basis of these techniques have been battle tested and proven by the standards of the Samurai.

The foremost authority on the subject and only other book ever written on the art form of Hojojutsu was Master Fujita Sieko.

During World War II, Fujita taught Nanban Sattō-ryū Kenpō in the Army Academy of Nakano (Rikugun Nakano Gakkō). Fujita later worked as a government security specialist, and continued the tradition of teaching Kōga-ryū Wada Ha style, among other martial arts. Notable students include Motokatsu Inoue, Mabuni Kenwa, Fujitani Masatoshi, actor Tomisaburo Wakayama and Manzo Iwata,

Fujita Seiko published *Zukai Torinawajutsu* showing hundreds of Hojōjutsu ties from many different schools, and several other texts on ninjutsu and martial arts. He died of cirrhosis of the liver at about the age of 68 and likely suffered from hereditary angioedema (which can preclude the practice of martial arts, although Fujita may have demonstrated the ability to overcome some disease symptoms). His collection, the *Fujita Seiko Bunko*, is housed at Iga-Ueno Museum in Odawara Castle, Japan.

Seiko went on to study several other martial arts and was also noted as an author, researcher and collector of ancient scrolls. According to some references, "opinions are divided if he was a real ninja or a mere <u>budō</u> researcher.

Use of the Hayanawa

The ideal for the Hayanawa was to apply it quickly with in ten seconds or less, skillfully, beautifully, and without risk of injury to the suspect. This rope was used only for apprehending suspects; because the person was not a convicted criminal prior to trial, no knots were used to avoid causing disgrace. In place of knots, the end of the rope was only looped under itself, and the constable kept the free end in hand.

Three "wrappings" with the Hayanawa

The Cross

With the loop end of the rope at Left of the back of the neck, bring the plain end through the loop and down, then around the Right upper arm, under the arm and across the back to Left arm; do the same there. Then bring the rope across the top of the horizontal to hold it in place, and through the part coming down from the neck (again on top of the horizontal). Pull

down. Then wrap the wrists (Right over Left) from top to bottom, from Left to Right and Right again, wrapping those 2 or 3 times. Then bring the free end under these wrappings, Left to Right. Hold the

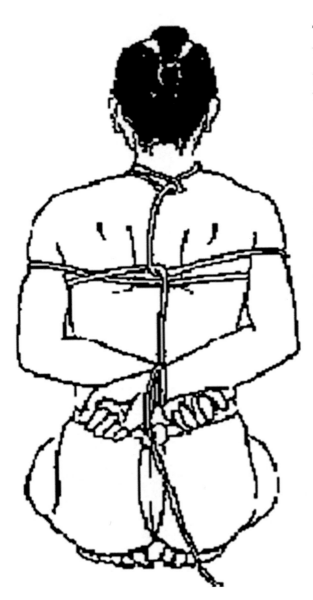

The Girdle or Diamond

The name is garnered form its shape. Double the rope and note the halfway point place this at the Adam's apple. Wrap the free ends around the back, crossing Left over Right, and wrap over the upper arms, Right and Left. Bring free ends around front and then pull through under the arms. Bring the two ends together at the lower back and pull taut. Wrap the wrists, Right over Left, as in the previous, keeping both ends together. Pass the ends under the Left side and pull through to Right to tighten.

The Well-curb Pass

The rope around the neck with the loop to the Right and pull taut. Bring the rope down diagonally to Left under the arm and wrap it over the Left upper arm. Pass the free end under the diagonal and pull it down to the Right, diagonally, under Right arm, over Right upper arm and under the second diagonal. Bring free end to small of back and wrap the wrists as in previous technique, 2 or 3 times. Pass the free end through from Left to Right. For all three of these, the back is the side for display. The front shows very little rope: only a single loop each at the neck and around each upper arm.

Note that these ties and bindings are only an example and are not taught with in this manual as a final submission or sublimation.

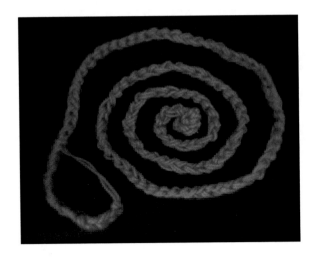

The Rope

The complexity of Hojojutsu was not purely in the advanced skill involved in executing the art form but it was also used as a means of communicating crucial information about the prisoners and their situations as different colored cord and different knot styles were used to display vital information.

The ropes came in several colors, the significance of which changed over time. According to the earliest tradition, which lasted into the Edo period (1603-1868), the basic colors that were associated with a well-established set of correspondences between seasons, directions, and the four Chinese (Shijin) guardian creatures of the four directions. The color of the rope changed with the season, and the prisoner was restrained facing the direction appropriate to the color and season. The correspondences were.

Blue: Spring-east (left) - blue dragon 2.

Red: Summer-south (front) - red phoenix 3.

White: Autumn-west (right)-white tiger 4.

Black: Winter-north (back)-black tortoise.

Yellow was used during the dog days of late July and early August.

The practice of using different colored ropes to indicate the severity of the criminal was of a low social standing and violet rope indicated a person of high rank.

By the end of the Edo period, the colors had been reduced to two, white and indigo, and their use corresponded not to seasons or directions but to the branch of the constabulary using the ropes. Hemp was used for the real ropes, but silk was used for practice, which was done with dummies made of straw or heavy Japanese paper. The Kaginawa was used to apprehend suspects by hooking the barb in the person's sash, collar, or if need bein the topknot, and then wrapping it around and around the body. The Hayanawa was also used to prevent escape. Unlike the Kaginawa, it had a small loop at one end, or sometimes a small metal ring. The plain end could be passed through this loop. For proper use it required the constable to be behind the suspect, or on horseback.

The ropes were made of strong hemp, but during practice silk alternatives were used which were bound around straw dummies or stacks of heavy paper.

Generally speaking two types of rope were used. Initially the fast rope or

Hayanawa was used to seize the criminal. This was a short thin rope (approximately 3-4mm) but was exceptionally strong. Occasionally the samurai would use the sageo that bound their sword sheaths for this purpose too. Once the Hayanawa rope was in place then the Torinawa was unleashed. The Torinawa (which translates as capture rope) was a lengthy piece of coiled rope that ensured the captive had significantly limited movement.

A Kaginawa (hooked rope) was often used to ensnare the captive before the rope binding process took place. The whole operation had to be very speedy and the dexterity needed was staggering. The Kaginawa was not intended to cause pain or injury, speed and beauty were integral to its skill. Its application should not have exceeded 10 seconds.

In this manual and for training purposes I have decidedly used the natural utility of the Japanese martial arts belt or Obi. The reasons are actually readily apparent but for clarification I will explain.

First: The easiest choice was because when I travel internationally to teach the techniques of Hojojutsu it is something that almost all martial arts students have available. The fact that it is such a singularly unique art form it is rare that other school and students of various martial arts have access to a rope specific to Hojojutsu in either the Torinawa or Honnowa form.

So it became a basic need to be able to teach to the masses with something that each student of various school and system would have at hand.

Second: Since my training in Hojojutsu there has always been the regular abrasions and rope burns that come with normal training periods in this art. To help eliminate and deter such painful injuries I found that the common martial arts or Karate belt has less friction and less abrasion when practicing. Thus, leading me again to teach with this form of material.

Third: The simple truth is that it is much more pliable and more user friendly than cord, rope or tie. Again leading me to use the simple and more affordable and accessible use of the martial arts rank belt. The cotton panels woven into the cloth of the belt makes it a softer and much easier way to learn for both your partner and yourself.

Technique and Skill

Hojojutsu transcends beyond being simply an effective method of restraining someone, being bound was meant to be highly humiliating and it was considered a very disrespectful act. Some say that even death was preferable than being a victim of Hojojutsu.

If multiple prisoners were restrained at once then they often were tied to one another. A variety of styles of knot were employed, some simply holding the prisoner in place while others progressively got tighter the more the prisoner struggled.

The most competent Hojojutsu artists have a great understanding of human anatomy and are able to execute knots in places that will suppress nerve sensation, numbing the extremities and causing temporary paralysis in this manner.

Hojojutsu is not only the art of using the rope to tie an opponent as a prisoner but also for defensive measures and sublimation of an attacker in short fast movements. The use of specific Musubi or special knots and twist ties of the rope or cord, the defender using Hojojutsu can manipulate the attacker in to various and general positions to ultimately detain and apprehend the attacker or subdue and sublimate the opponent in a capture technique or maneuver.

In the art of Hojojutsu the most used technique and what any practical student of the form should practice most are the intricate and subtle knots or Musubi that can be quickly applied and tied in swift movements.

Within each System that teaches the Art of Hojojutsu or portions therein you will find a full range of Musubi techniques that will capture and detain an attacker with great ease.

The simplified movements that you can find in this manual are only a few of the many musubi ties that help apply and sublimate an opponent with skill. These ties can only be learned with many hours

and even years of practice to master or begin to understand the complexity of each Musubi knot.

Many of the techniques in this book use a simplified Musubi as a capture technique against an attacker.

The techniques in this manual are a conglomeration of several schools of training from a variety of different teachers and is not a specific style or school of practice of traditional Hojojutsu. They are my personal approach to this subject matter and finding on the art form and its history.

I consider it my duty and privilege to be the historian of the current generation and to forward all my collective learning and knowledge on to others. One of the many amazing arts that I have trained in first hand and found to be an enrichment to my martial education is the Hojojutsu art. One which I now pass on to you the reader to enjoy and study at your own discretion.

Please practice all techniques with the three rules of training.

Slowly, Safely and securely

"New eras don't come about because of swords, they are created by the people who wield them."
~ Nobuhiro Watsuki

*NOTE *that this art has been used for such purposes and can easily restrict breathing and brain/blood activity and must be applied with all caution in training and or application.*

Chapter 2

Bind Us in Unity

There are so many variations and styles of Jujutsu that have taught the Hojojutsu techniques that are as unique as the arts they are derived form. For this reason it should be noted that the techniques in this book that follow are my interpretation only. The ties and knots and complex defense movements that I teach both in my international seminars and those that can be found in my books and DVDs are the techniques I have been taught from separate arts. In development of my own Hojojutsu these techniques are my own personal practices for the defensive aspects of the arts that I teach. You can research more for yourself on the traditional art of Hojojutsu and the binding art they serve.

Hojojutsu Today

Although the demise of the Samurai has led to Hojojutsu becoming a dying art, there are still a few martial art experts who are adept in the skill. Not only is it still taught by a select few instructors but is still used by the Japanese police currently. They carry lengths of rope with them as well as handcuffs. They are only allowed to employ this device if they are sufficiently skilled in the art of Hojojutsu.

In many traditional schools you are able to train in Hojojutsu only after completing specific levels of mastery with in their respective system. Hojojutsu is only a compartment of a traditional Jujitsu system or school of learning. Because of the complexity of the Hojojutsu system it should be noted that most students train for years to study the basic fundamentals of Jujutsu to understand footwork and techniques that will be used in the Hojojutsu training.

The Society of Hojojutsu

There are a few select clubs throughout Japan that offer Hojojutsu instruction, it is still considered a very specialist art and training is intense and specific. It is an exceptionally beautiful art to observe and the speed in which the capture is completed is breathtaking. Demonstrations of Hojojutsu are more common now that the law of secrecy has relaxed and are certainly worth attending as it really is an experience you need to witness first hand to understand the true wonder of this ancient art form.

I have chosen to initiate the start of the first International Hojojutsu Society so that others may learn, train and share the unique and various portions of this art form with others. The association or *Sei* is open to all interested parties and anyone can become a member and share their interest and select style with others within the society. Feel free to contact the Society for more information at the end of this book.

"BIND US IN UNITY"

The Motto for the International Hojojutsu Society

International Hojojutsu Society we openly share and learn from one another the intricacies of the fundamental understanding of different approaches and musubi that are used in select and unique techniques.

The Society also is in place to additionally train and instruct in the understanding of the basic use and skill of Hojojutsu and can thereby certify such individuals to teach the techniques and basic knowledge of Hojojutsu. The society is there to help and support other practitioners as well as create a harmony between various styles and training systems of the art of Hojojutsu.

Today's Hojojutsu Begins

Because there are countless systems and various subsections of Hojojutsu and therein the countless Musubi or knots to learn there is no one that is known currently that understands and has knowledge of them all. Within the

In the research of traditional Hojojutsu you have to begin understanding the nature of Hojojutsu itself. The art of Binding and that of traditional Japanese Hojojutsu can be found in ancient scrolls and depicted in various paintings and art renderings over hundreds of years of Japanese cultural and heretical influence.

Hojojutsu is an art form that is merely a compartment to a traditional Japanese Jujutsu system. The movements and techniques can be found in various systems such as but not limited to Danzen Ryu, Hakko Ryu and Daito systems. The traditional Hojojutsu art form and techniques can be broken down to several groups and select portions such as the Torinawa and Honnowa. The Art or more so the development of the portion of Hojojutsu that are found most interesting and useful for me have always been the Hayanawa or *fast rope* techniques that are used as a defensive measure against an assailant or attacker.

Hojojutsu shows limited survival in the modern world, both in Japan and elsewhere. Torinawa-techniques are taught as part of the curriculum learned by modern Japanese police officers and it remains an advanced topic within schools of jujutsu, following it and other Japanese traditional martial arts as they make their way around the world from Brazil to Eastern Europe.

Although the Honnawa techniques have long been supplanted by handcuffs and leg-irons, some teachers of traditional martial arts in Japan work to continue to maintain the art form. The Soke (head of, and heir to the style) of Masaki-ryu Bujutsu, Nawa Yumio, has written several books on the subject and has worked as a historical consultant on matters dealing with law-enforcement and Mizukoshi Hiro's recently reprinted book *Torinawajutsu* offers historical background followed by thorough, practical instruction in more than 25 traditional ties including some recreated from rare and very old texts. The Koryu cited are Seigo Ryu Jujutsu, Seishin Ryu Jujutsu, Koden Enshin Ryu Iaijutsu, Nanbu Handen Hojo Jutsu, Kurokawa Ryu , Mitsuo (Mippa) Muteki Ryu, Bo Ryu and Tenfu Muso Ryu. Although long out-of-print, the late Seiko Fujita's monumental work, *Zukai Torinawajutsu* could be considered a bible of the art; showing hundreds of ties from many different schools.

In this book you will find the Ninjutsu, Kurama Yoshin Ryu Jujutsu, basic principles and techniques used in the devise of Hojojutsu. These are techniques that can be found in various portions of Hojojutsu such as the Hayanawa, Torinawa and Kaginawa.

Through the practice of the techniques is should be noted that students and those attempting to learn the techniques in this manual should practice the three basic rules of training. These training techniques will help to promote less injury and safety while learning step by step movements. These three tips are

Safely, Securely and Slowly. Utilizing the three steps to study you can help prevent and manage the levels of pain and discomfort during the practice of these techniques. When working with a partner you should at all times do each technique and maneuver Safely, Securely and Slowly so that you can clearly understand how each step functions as a part of the whole as well as helping your training partner and that of the person being submitted to be tied and held with an individual technique without the suffering that comes with such maneuvers. Many techniques wrap around the neck and throat and can cause damage and asphyxia (Choke out/ Loss of breath) and even in some stages permanent injury and possible death.

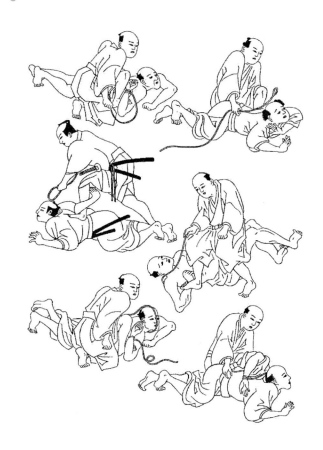

"Practice slowly, safely and securely."

~ Allen Woodman

Chapter 3

Rear Choke Attack #1

Ippon Seoi Nage

In this section we begin learning and understanding a few of the intricate moves and positions to gain defense against an attacker from various angles and attacks. I once again urge each student and practitioner to follow the three words of training, that of Safety, Securely and slowly for the sake of comfort and caution when practicing so that you may find a happy and safe medium in which both Ate (or attacking practice partner) and Uke (Throwing / Falling student)

may both enjoy and learn the technique with limited risk and enjoyable study together for mutual benefit.

Ippon Seoi Nage

Rear Attack

(Choke hold from the rear)

Single Arm Shoulder Throw

The attacker begins by grasping around the neck from the rear. Pulling inward causing a choke or rear naked choke. The defense would not change the approach if attack is with both hands.

1. a. 1.b The defender stands in a natural position as the attacker grabs around neck creating.

2. a 2.b The defender raises the rope (Belt) upwards and throws it rearward and around the back of attackers head and neck region.

3 A fast snap outward penetrates a strike to the attacker's neck.

4. a 4.b Sliding the left foot backwards and to the side of attackers leg. Dropping to the left knee and pulling the attacker over his back and to the ground.

5. a 5.b 5.c. Using the ends of each side of the rope (Belt) Crossing around the face and bridge of the nose causes severe pain and discomfort to the attacker.

4.b.

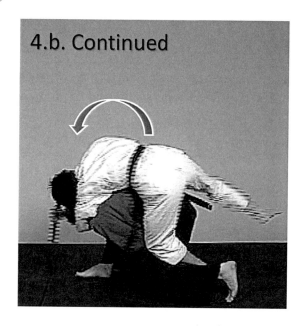

4.b. Continued

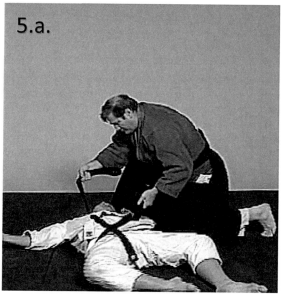

5.a.

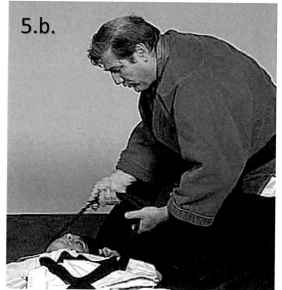

5.b.

5.c.

In this position the attacker can be sublimated by a quick catch and thread looping knot. Known as Musubi the restraint allows for the defender to apply pressure to the neck arm face and head. This hold also will allow for control of the opponent as well. With pulling or pushing movements against the cord or rope application the defender can turn and/ or roll the opponent over toward their front in a prone position facing downward. Crossing the cord/belt across the face upon the jaw line and bridge of the nose creates a painful restraint to the attacker. Cross the ropes and both sides across the face and head. This creates pressure on the attacker's skull and jaw bone that can fracture the bone or separate the jawbone from the mandible placement. Please be extra cautious when attempting this technique or during practice with a partner. Remember that any form of strikes can also be implemented to subdue or halt an attacker at this point.

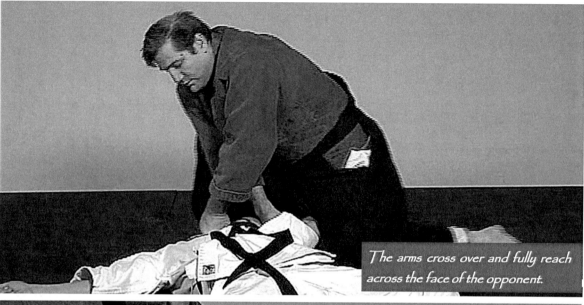

The arms cross over and fully reach across the face of the opponent.

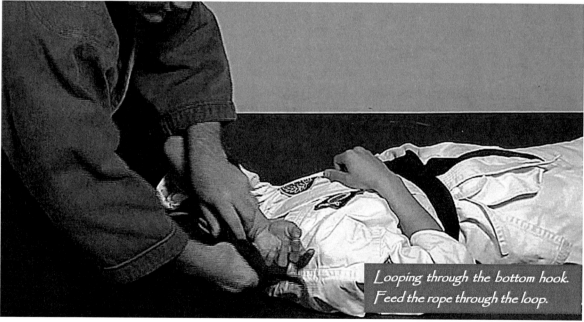

Looping through the bottom hook. Feed the rope through the loop.

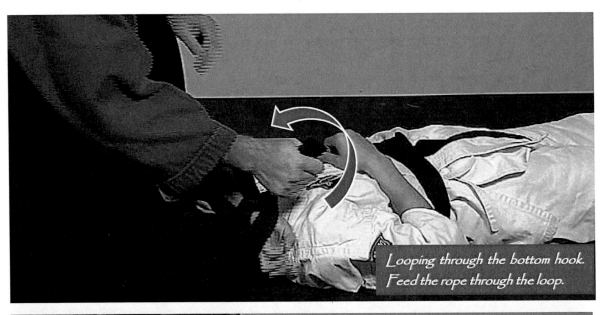

Looping through the bottom hook. Feed the rope through the loop.

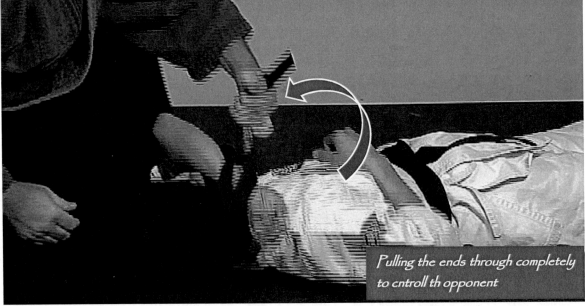

Pulling the ends through completely to cntroll th opponent

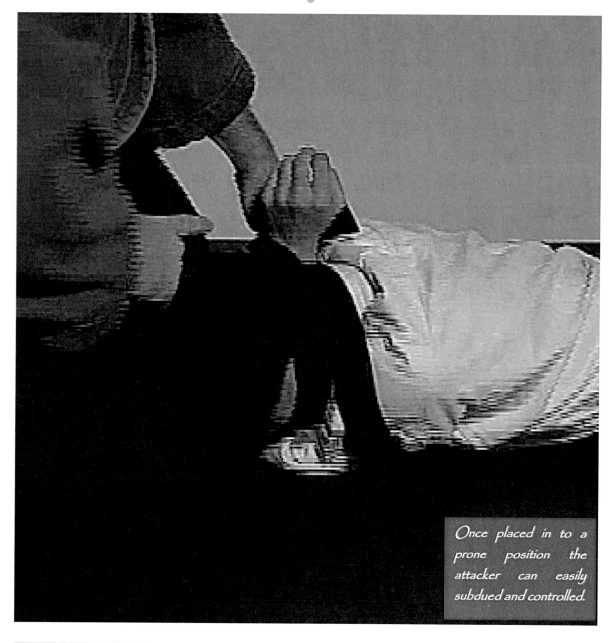

Once placed in to a prone position the attacker can easily subdued and controlled.

Chapter 4

Rear Choke Attack #2

Shiho Nage Waza

Rear Attack

(Choke hold / Strike)

Shiho Nage Waza

Outward arm twisting defense

This attack is from behind and from the same as the previous position.

1. As the attacker grabs the defender from behind in a choke or neck control movement, the defender turns inward toward the opponent. This position opens the defender up from the grasp of the assailant.

2. The defender then can thrust or whip the cord or belt toward the attackers face and head. In a hard and deliberate throw of the cord or belt the defensive movement will immediately loosen the grasp of any attacker allowing for the following step to be easily applied.

Striking the face and head of the attacker automatically releases the grip of the opponent on the defender and allows for freedom of some movement.

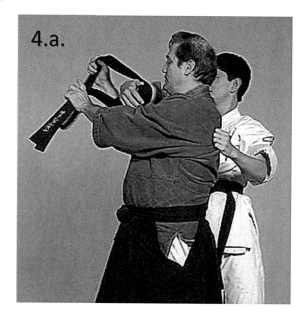

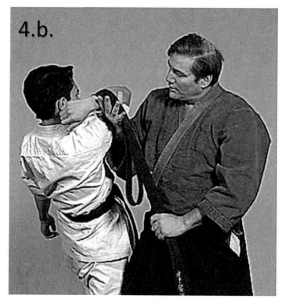

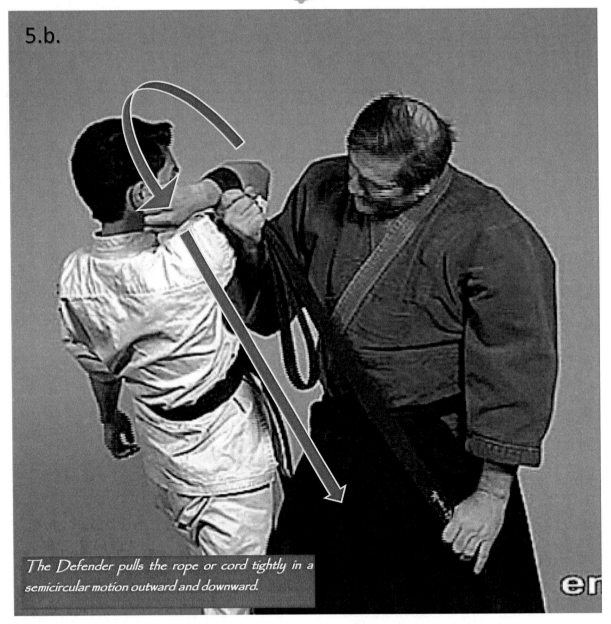

5.b.

The Defender pulls the rope or cord tightly in a semicircular motion outward and downward.

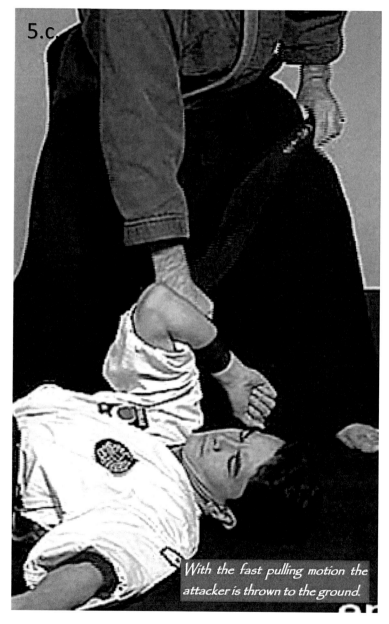

5.c.

With the fast pulling motion the attacker is thrown to the ground.

3. In this movement the belt or cord loop slips inward and down. Through the attackers grip and to the wrist.

4.a. With a single continuing motion the defenders body should adjust to a 180°degree position to the outside (right) of the opponent.

4.b. Continuing in a nonstop manner with the held ends of the cord or rope moved behind the attackers body. At this juncture the defender will grasp the ends together and begin to slip tie and catch the rope to capture the wrist of the attacker.

5.a. The defender will simply pull downward in a slightly circular pattern to create a throw to disable the attacker and create a capture technique.

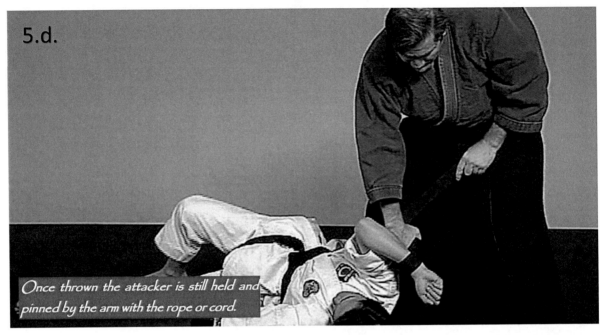

5.d.

Once thrown the attacker is still held and pinned by the arm with the rope or cord.

5.b. – 5.d. From the ground position the defender can easily sublimate the opponent.

When practicing the techniques remember to adjust the rope as you throw the opponent downward. By pulling the slack from the rope with the left hand the grip will tighten around opponent's wrist and subdue opponent. Follow through with a diagonal and circular movement to pull the opponent off balance creating the throw.

With any suggested technique in Hojojutsu the ultimate goal and result should end with a restraint of the attacker. As in any techniques in Hojojutsu there are several paths to this end. Once the position has been obtained the defender can use several techniques to complete the restraint and totally disarm and subdue the attacker.

6. In this series of sublimation techniques the defender throws the rope or cord around the neck and face of the attacker now in a supine position.

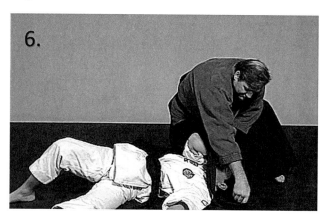

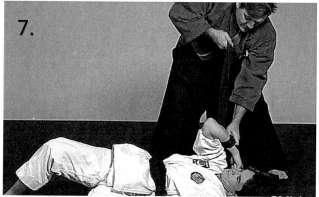

7. Pulling the slack up and then around in a smooth movement will bind the opponents arm to his upper shoulder area and neck.

8. By easily pulling the rope or cord with the right hand can turn the attacker toward his stomach to both better protect yourself from further attacks and also place the opponent in a submissive and supine position.

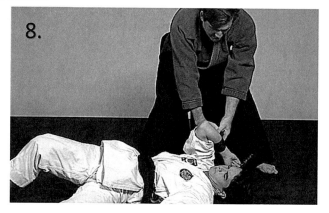

9. Once the rope or cord is wrapped around the head of the attacker pull upwards to constrain the attacker's arms and head to bind together. Cinching the rope or belt upward creates a strong and abrasive hold for an attacker. This allows the defender to gain an advantage over his /her opponent.

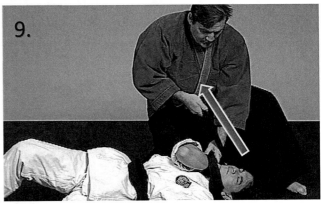

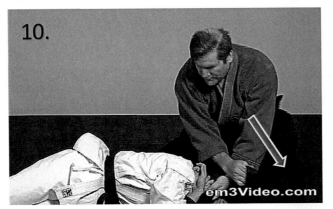

10. Once puled tightly the defender can then push / Pull the rope or cord to roll the attacker to a prone position and final sublimation.

11. Ultimately the position of the defender will sit over the head of the prone attacker. This technique will not allow for movement or struggle while the rope or cord is applied in a slip knot or holding position.

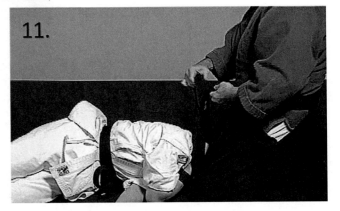

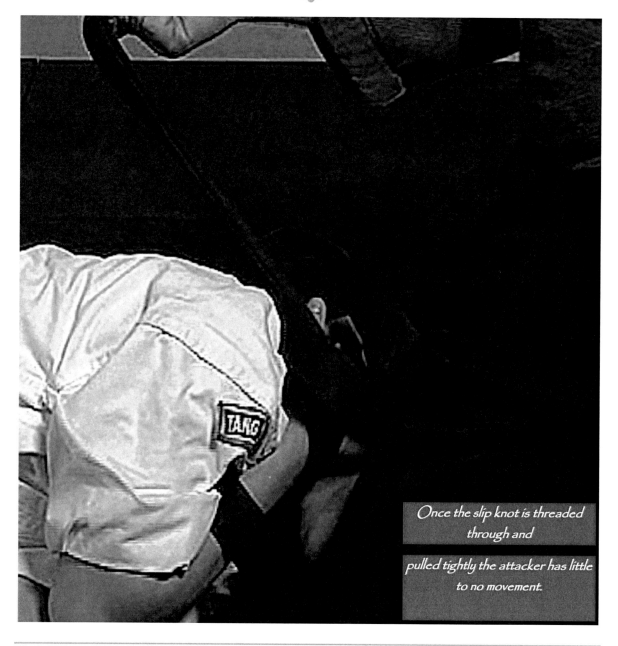

Once the slip knot is threaded through and

pulled tightly the attacker has little to no movement.

Chapter 5

Front Punch Attack #1

Shibari Ude Uke

From a forward attack or a lunge punch

Front Punch Attack #1

(Arm twist and lock)

Shibari Ude Uke

Arm Twist and arm bar lock and restraint.

This attack is presented from a front punch or a frontal attack. It is a direct attack without any suggestion of slipping the punch or a fast returned jab.

The defender is in a natural and relaxed stance.

1. As the attacker strikes in with a forward lung punch or strike, the defender rotates his body to a 90° angle to the attack. As the defender rotates to the outside the rope or cord is used to deflect any residual arm movement form the attack and blocking the strike simultaneously. In this action and for this specific technique the defender should have the right arm raised and the left arm lower than the attackers elbow.

2. Once the strike has been deflected or blocked the defender will move his arms in opposing direction. The right arm of the defender moves down and over the attackers arm as the left arm simultaneously.

3. This single movement creates a quick capture technique and applies a basic arm bar to the attackers striking arm.

4. Creating an arm bar technique can be a finishing technique as the result can be a painful broken arm or dislocated elbow joint.

5. The defender moves and slides the rope and catch position outward toward the attackers wrist. 5.a.-5.c.

Using a circular motion the defender then begins to rotate the ropes and arms of the opponent toward the back of the attacker. The defenders position will end up directly behind the opponent with an applied arm lock or chicken wing position. This motion is carried through the forwarding 3 individual photos. 5.d. -5.f.

1.

Using the rope or cord to parry or deflect the attack

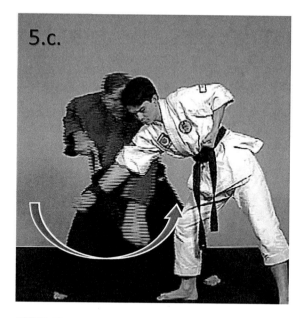

Note that in this position the rope or cord is drawn across each other and holds the arm in a secure position from the rear.

6. Sliding the rope through the hand and fingers the defender will begin the warp around the neck and throat of the attacker while still holding the arm hold in the rear.

7. As the defender wraps around the neck of the attacker the loop (held in the right hand) will be open to thread the ends of the Left hands Cord or rope ends. Threading the rope creating a fast Musubi or knot tie. 7.a.-7.e.

5.f. Opposite view

The rope or cord is used to create and

Arm bar or chicken wing hold.

6.

The defender's hand slips downward toward the rope end or loop.

7.a.

Grabbing and opening the loop end of the rope or cord will allow a strong hold for the defender.

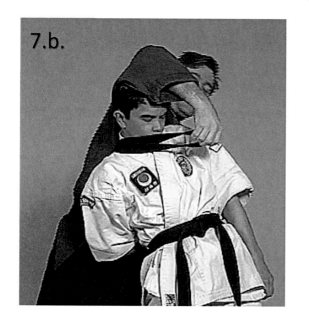

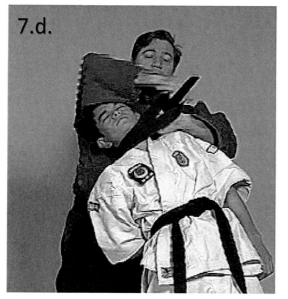

7.e. Close up

7.d.-7.e. Threading the rope or cord through the loop makes a quick catch and tie that allows only one hand to be used. Thus freeing the other hand of the defender for further possible attacks from either the assailant or other parties. Throwing the opponent down and back.

8.

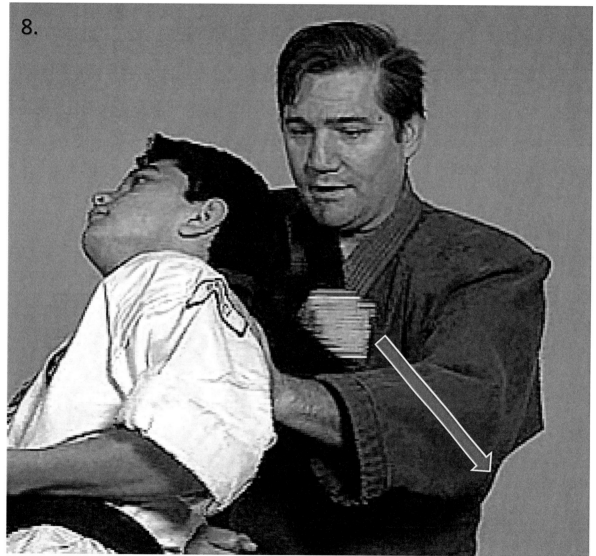

8.   A quick pull to the rear of the attacker will force the opponent off balance and create a backwards throw. Throwing the opponent to the ground.

9.

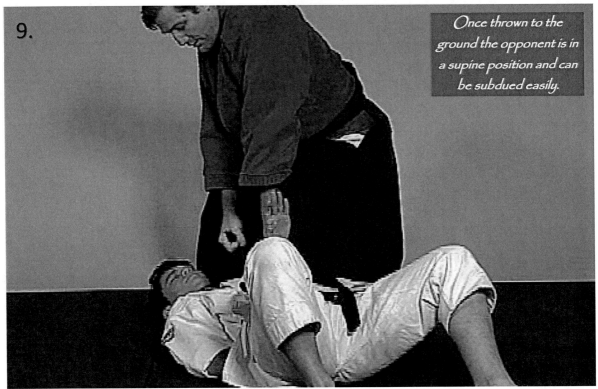

Once thrown to the ground the opponent is in a supine position and can be subdued easily.

9.   When the cord has been threaded through the loop it is a simple pull downward and backward to drag the assailant backwards and to the ground.

Note of caution during this technique as the opponents hand is still trapped behind his own back and during the fall this can injure and possibly break or dislocate the arm or elbow.

Please use special caution when practicing this movement to insure the safety of your partner.

Remember that in this final position above the techniques of apprehension can be applied as before. Sublimating the opponent in a prone position to bind them for detainment.

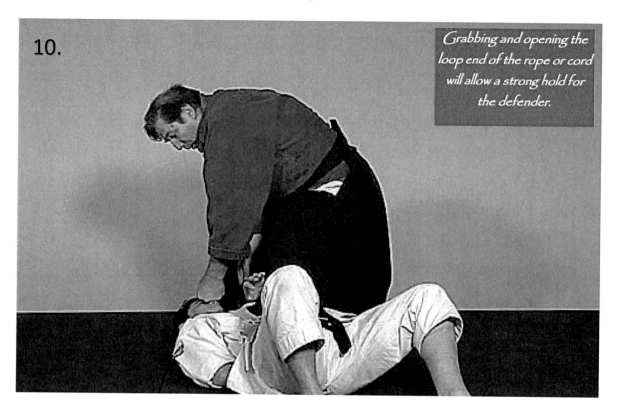

10.

Grabbing and opening the loop end of the rope or cord will allow a strong hold for the defender.

10. Once the attacker has fallen further techniques can be applied to subdue and sublimate the attacker in a complete form.

Note that the left leg shields the defender from attacks or retaliation from the opponent. The left leg should be placed against the arm and shoulder area of the attackers left arm to negate such attacks.

From here other strikes can also be delivered such as Shuto (Knife Hand), Ippon Ken (Knuckle strike) or Ken (Straight Punch.)

Chapter 6

Front Punch Attack #2

Kote Kubi Nage

Reverse Punch Attack #2

Kote Kubi Nage

Wrist Catch and Neck Throw

In this technique the defender has an extended length of rope or cord in hand.

This technique uses the length to defend and capture the opponent.

This photo demonstrates the proper placement of the hands and rope or cord as well as the body position and arm position of the defender. Note that the forearm is also in contact with the attackers arm or strike as it comes forward. The rope helps to deflect or parry the attack but it is the left forearm itself that is actually blocking the incoming strike in this position.

1. As the attack comes forward the defender uses the previous defense of moving to a 90° angle to the attack. Using the rope or cord to deflect the attack at the angle. In this defense unlike the previous defensive technique the left hand of the defender is in an upward position and the defenders right hand is down and below the attackers elbow.

2. The defenders right hand (lower than the attacker's arm) raises upward and wraps the attackers wrist.

3. The defender simultaneously wraps the left handed held cord or rope around the head and neck of the attacker from front to back. Fully encircling the attackers head and neck creating a choke and strong grip.

4. As the rope is wrapped fully around the opponent using a cinch to create a loop in the right hand, the rope or cord is also fast looped in the left hand as it is fed through the right hand loop.

5. The rope or cord loop is now switched to the other hand. As the defender drops to his left knee.

6. As the defender keeps grip with the hand held loop in his left hand and rope to his left knee, the defender pulls strongly on the rope or cord falling (Throwing) the attacker over the defenders shoulder.

7. This is a reverse view of the rear hold and position.

8. Another reverse angle of the thread through loop.

View from opposite side.

5.a. From this view point you can see the defender is creating the loop by pulling through the cinch loop in the opposite hand.

At this point the Musubi Is fully   tied and in place.

This technique can be done quickly and easily however, it does take practice to master this quick capture technique to be applied at full speed.

As with all Martial Arts techniques and more over the techniques throughout this text book the intricate detail and proper positioning during a techniques performance must be practiced multiple times and with repetitive actions to improve one's skill level and ability to properly utilize any of the techniques in this manual.

5.b. Thread through the loop as the defender pulls the cord or rope to a cinched tie.

5.b. View from opposite side.

From this point you can grip the loop in the left hand and pull to tighten the Masubi loop.

6.a.

In this series of photos the defender is using the loop held in hand to pull forcefully over the defender' shoulder.

Please note that this technique is a full throwing technique that can easily injure your training partner and should be practiced with in safe and controlled restraint in your practice.

6.a. Pulling the opponent over the shoulder and back of the defender. Once the opponent has been thrown successfully over the shoulder, creating a throw to the attacker. The defender has the option to strike the attacker with any of the aforementioned techniques of such as Shuto (Knife Hand), Ippon Ken (Knuckle strike) or Ken (Straight Punch.) 6.a.-6.c.

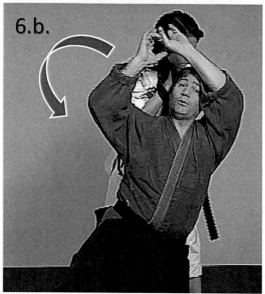

6.b.

6.c.

Once thrown the defender can subdue the assailant or strike with standard punches or knife hand strikes.

Chapter 7

Front Punch Attack #3

Kote Gaeishi Bogyo

Front Punch Attack #3

Kote Gaeishi Bogyo

Wrist twist and throw defense

The defender begins in a relaxed and natural position. The cord/ belt/ rope is held with both hands in an uncollected manner.

1. As the attacker strikes in with a forward motion and punch. The defender as before turns 90° outside the opponents attack. The rope or cord used as a deflector for the attack. Outside the attackers arm.

2. The defender wraps the cord or rope upward and around the attacker's wrist creating a capture.

3. With the right hand placed behind the opponents hand and wrist the defender grasp to control the attackers hand.

3.b The wrist grab from a different angle. Gripping the wrist and hand together.

4.a. The defender uses a circular stepping movement (Tenkan). The step is a rotation of the defenders body to an inside position.

4.b As the defender circles in a stepping motion, the wrist grab begins rotating in a circular motion to create the oncoming throw. As seen in photos 5-5.d

5.a.

Stepping back in to a turning step creates a dynamic throw and capture.

5.b.

Using the wrist to help create the throwing technique is the key.

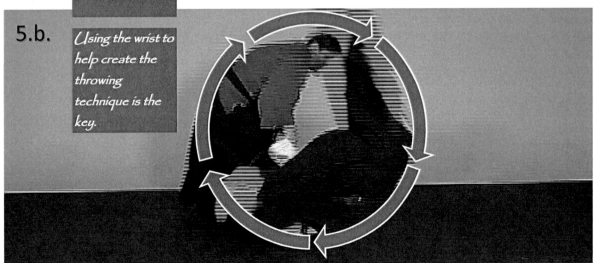

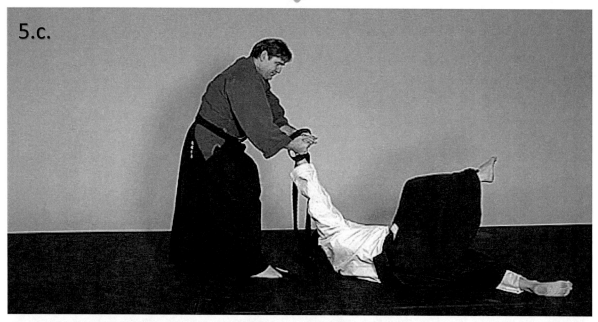

5.c.

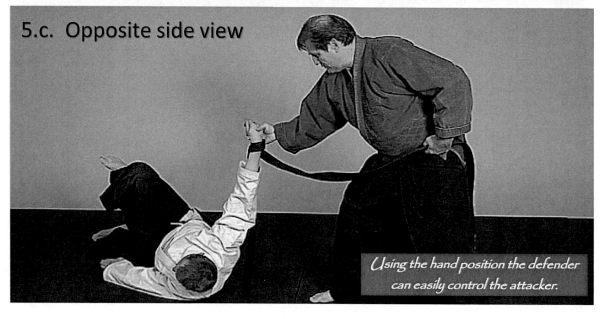

5.c. Opposite side view

Using the hand position the defender can easily control the attacker.

6 Once the throw has been completed the defender uses the attackers on arm to pin and rotate the opponent's body in to position.

7 Using the wrist lock and the attackers own arm the defender rotates the opponent over to the prone position.

8 Rotate the attacker's arm to their back. Creating an arm bar or chicken wing. The rope will remain behind the wrist automatically. Keep the rope behind the wrist position. Using the rope or cord pull upward to tighten the hold of the attacker's arm.

9 Grab the attacker's free hand (left hand) and place it behind his back.

10 Defender places the attacker's left hand on top of right hand. Bring the opponents left hand to the back and over the already held right hand of attacker.

11 Allow the rope or cord to wrap over both hands. Over the top of both hands of opponent. 11.a.-11.c.

12 The defenders right hand slips under the left arm of the opponent to easily grasp the free rope or cord. As the defenders arm reaches through and grasps the rope or cord. The defender pulls the rope or cord through and under both of the opponent's hands. 12.a.-12.d

13 As the defenders right hand pulls the cord through the rope or cord is also pulled through the cord or rope that is held by the left hand of the defender. This creates a simple Musubi or cinch tie that traps the opponent's hands in position. 13.a-13.e.

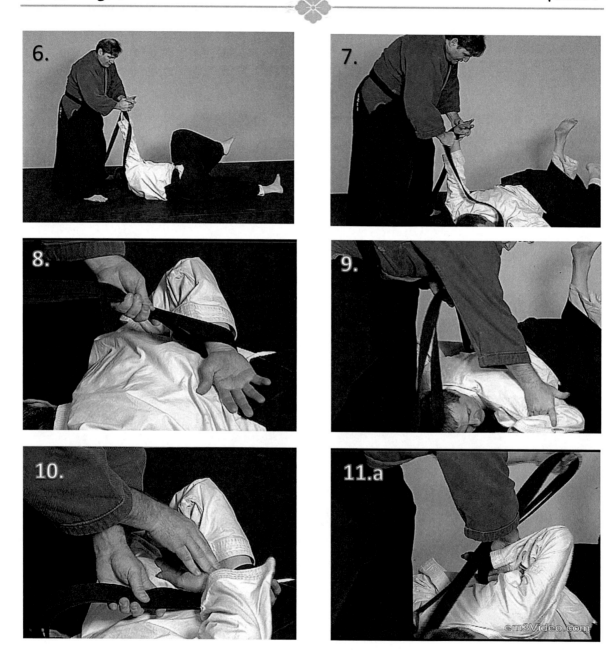

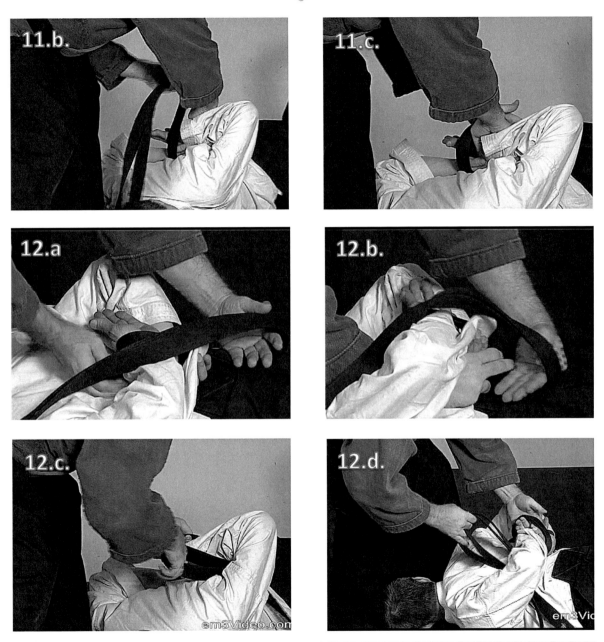

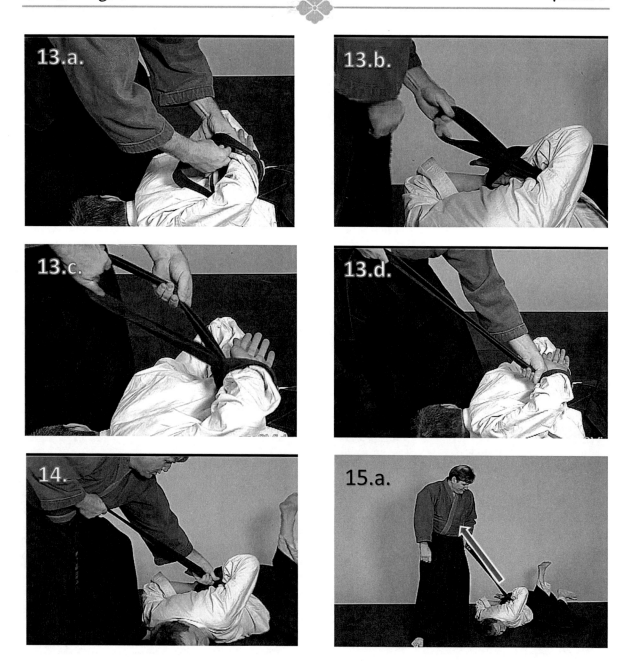

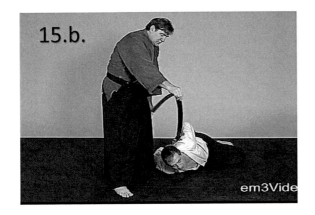

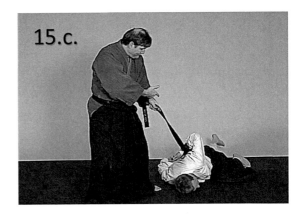

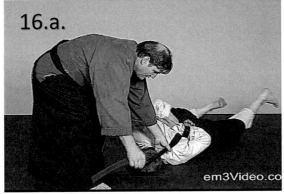

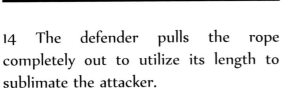

14 The defender pulls the rope completely out to utilize its length to sublimate the attacker.

15 once the rope or cord is fully extended it is possible to use the length of rope or cord to hold the attacker's body in a pinned positon. 15.a.-15c.

16. By placing the rope or cord on the ground at the defenders feet and stepping with full weight on the rope. This applies force to the rope or cord. 16.a.-16.b

Chapter 8

Front Kick Defense #1

Mae Geri Bogyo

Front Kick Defense #1

Mae Geri Bogyo

Stop Kick and Drop

This defense is utilized when an attack is forthcoming by way of kicking.

1. In this series the defender once again is in a relaxed and natural position. As the opponent lunges forward with a front kick. (Either leg can be used.) the rope or cord is folded upon itself and the loop is on the defenders right hand.

2. The defender uses a snapping technique to stop the attack and cause pain to the attacker. 2.a.-2.d.

2.b. Snapping motion

Using the cord or rope in a snapping manner to stop the power of the strike.

The main key element to this technique is the snap of the rope or cord downward. This applied technique of snapping creates more power and speed to allow enough force to be applied to ensure that the kick is stopped and halted from its forward and upward motion.

2.c. Snapping motion from different view.

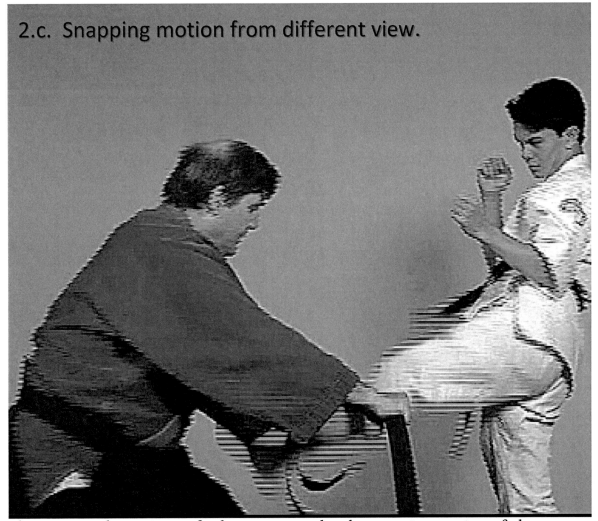

This is another view of the same technique. The kick is stopped by the downward motion and the power created by the snapping motion of the rope or cord.

2.d. Snapping motion from opposite view.

This technique can easily injure the leg /foot/ankle of the opponent. Please be careful when practicing this technique. From the opposite viewpoint. It is clear to see the kick can be stopped proficiently. Note that at the same time as the kick is presented by the attacker the defender also steps backwards to diffuse the power and intention of the kick.

3. After the kick has been stopped the following move is presented without interruption. The rope is held at face / neck level. The defender moves with both ends forward and up to the attackers head and face.

4. Wrapping both hands and following with a forward motion against the attacker. The defender pushes forward and wraps the cord or rope around the attackers head.

5. Once the cord or rope is wrapped around the defender grabs both ends of the cord or rope with a single hand. This allows the defender to have a single hand free for defense against further attacks either from the opponent or an outward attack from someone else.

6. With the cord or rope wrapped firmly around the head and hands of the attacker the defender pulls downward and backward creating a throw. The opponent is pulled forcefully off balance and thrown backwards.

7. When the assailant is forced down and falls or is thrown to their back the defender can strike the opponent easily with either hand strikes or kicking strikes to finish off the opponent.

8. This photo demonstrates the kicks and strikes that can be applied form this position. In this photo the kick is a stomp to the groin of the attacker.

9. This Kick demonstrates a heal kick to the sternum or stomach of the opponent.

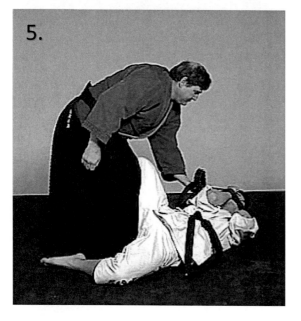

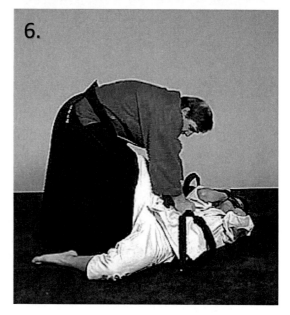

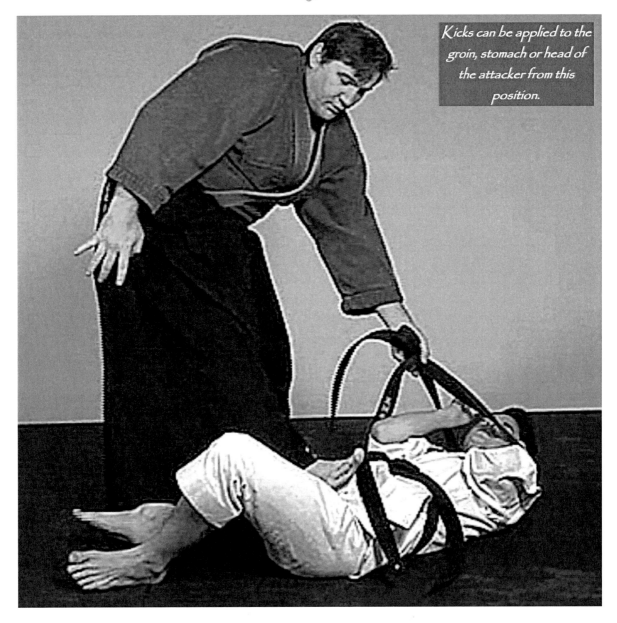

Kicks can be applied to the groin, stomach or head of the attacker from this position.

Kicks can be applied to the groin, stomach or head of the attacker from this position.

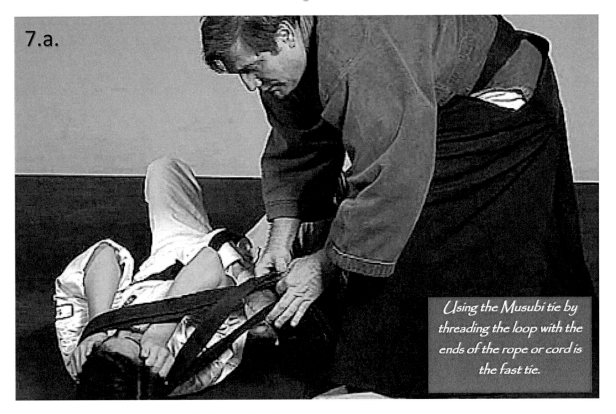

7.a.

Using the Musubi tie by threading the loop with the ends of the rope or cord is the fast tie.

7.a.   By stepping forward the defender can grasp the loop end and feed the loose ends through. Creating a fast tie or Musubi that when pulled can easily hold the assailant.

7.b. Feed the rope or cord through the loop in the defenders left hand.

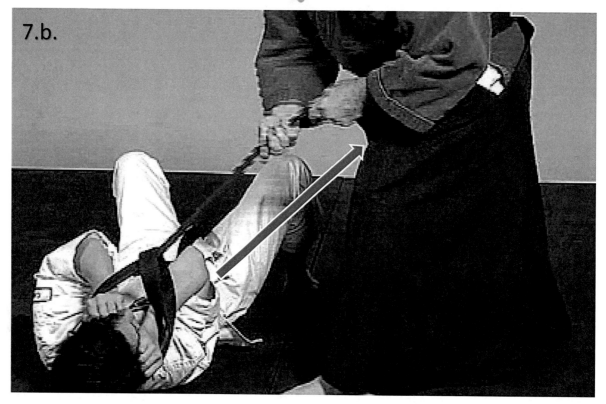

7.b.

7.c. The threading of the rope or cord once pulled tightly produces a quick catch Musubi tie that will restrain the assailant fast. From this position simply stepping back and pulling the cord or rope binds the rope against the hands and face of the attacker.

The following photos depict the action and ease of the technique to subdue the attacker.

7.c.

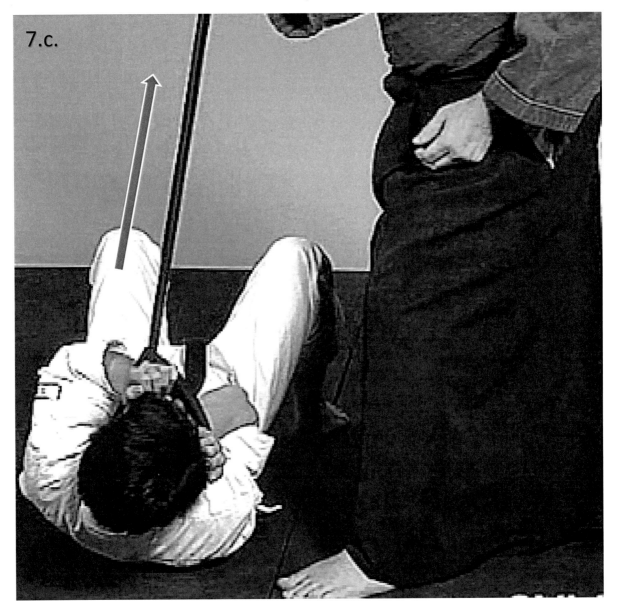

8 The final position allows for control and submission of the attacker as well opens other avenues of sublimation using the cord or rope to wrap and bind the attacker.

Chapter 9

Double Punch Attack #1

Nidai Zuki Ikkyo Bogyo

Double Punch Attack #1

Nidai Zuki Ikkyo Bogyo

(Double punch defense with Arm Twist)

This technique is developed using the length of the rope or cord.

The rope is open and held in a non-belligerent way and somewhat natural position.

1. The defender uses the similar parry block with the hand held rope or cord in both hands. Blocking and deflecting the attack from the outside position. 1.a.-1.d.

Photo 1.c. is a view form the opposite side for a better look at the technique and the advantage it presents.

1.d. Opposite view, in this photo you can see the parry block using the rope or cord to deflect the attack as it enters.

2.a. Staying in position and in place the defender waits for the second attack to come. As the attack approaches the defender uses the same deflection block with the hand held rope or cord.

2.b. The opposite view for the deflection and parry technique.

3   As the assailant continues the circular movement of the attack, the defender allows the movement to follow through. The deflecting block of the rope is then wrapped from behind the attacker's hand with the defender's right hand and rope still firmly held in the right hand. The wrap is done quickly by looping the rope or cord around and over the attackers punching hand (Left Hand) 3.a.-3.b.

3.c. From the starting viewpoint the attackers hand is wrapped with the defender's rope or cord.

4   The defender moves slightly with a circular turning motion to the attacker's outside position. As the rope is wrapped around   the attackers striking hand, the defender slides the right hand downward holding lightly to the rope or cord.

5   As the defender holds the rope or cord with the right hand, the defender can begin to wrap the rope around the arm (forearm and toward the shoulder). Begin wrapping the rope or cord around and upwards toward the attacker's shoulder and above the opponents elbow joint location. The defenders left hand should be held at one point against the wrist of the attackers' hand and not moved. 5.a.-5.b.

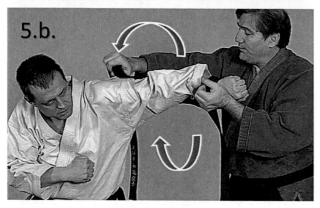

Keeping contact with the attacker's wrist is paramount to the success of this technique.

This point is specifically important to the understanding of the technique in practical application. The defender's left hand should stay in constant contact with the attacker's wrist or back of hand. This contact is a trapping maneuver that keeps the opponent from moving away or outwards in an attempt to dislodge the technique from being applied.

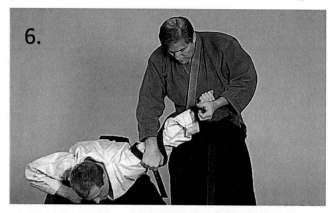

6 While wrapping the opponent over the arm and toward the shoulder, the defender takes a small step forward to create what is known as a 1kkyo technique (First position), the defender's right hand still holds the cord or rope and travels along the outside of the arm creating the arm lock and spin of the attacker's arm.

7 The continued motion of the forward step moves the assailant to the ground in a prone position. 7.a.-7.b.

8 The defender swings the arm of the opponent backward and to the rear position creating an arm bar or chicken wing maneuver. 8.a.-8b.

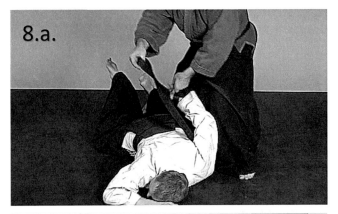

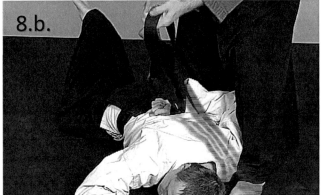

9 Reaching out with the right hand the defender grabs the assailant's right arm and brings the arm toward the back to trap the arm in an additional arm bar or chicken wing.

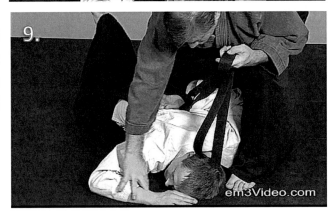

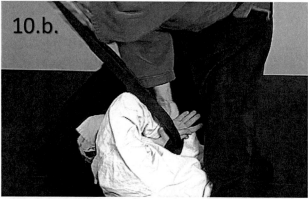

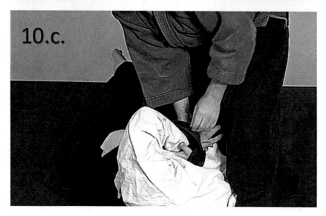

10   The attacker's left hand is placed on top of the opponent's right hand already constricted with the cord n din a resting and holding position. As the attacker's hand is brought to the back the defender brings the rope or cord over the top of both of assailant's hands and/or wrist. 10.a.-10.c.

11 The defender reaches through and under the opponents arm. Grasping the rope or cord and pulling it through the arm of the attacker. 11.a-11.c.

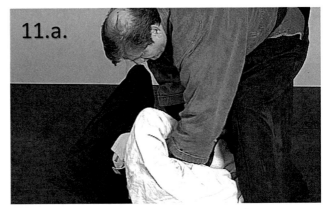

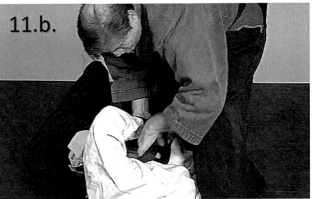

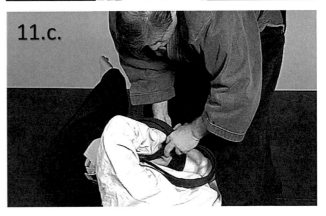

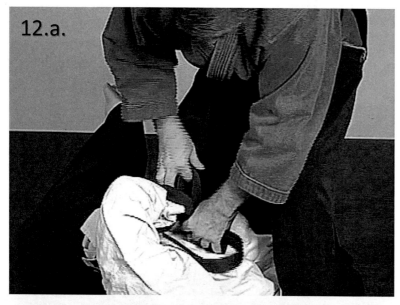

12.a.

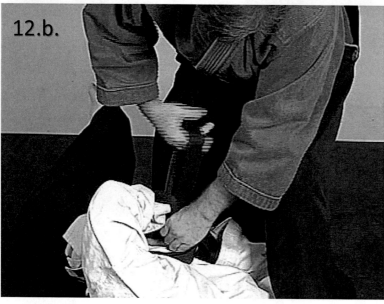

12.b.

12 Once the cord is pulled through the attacker's arm then thread the rope or cord through itself to form a basic Musubi tie. 12.a.-12.c.

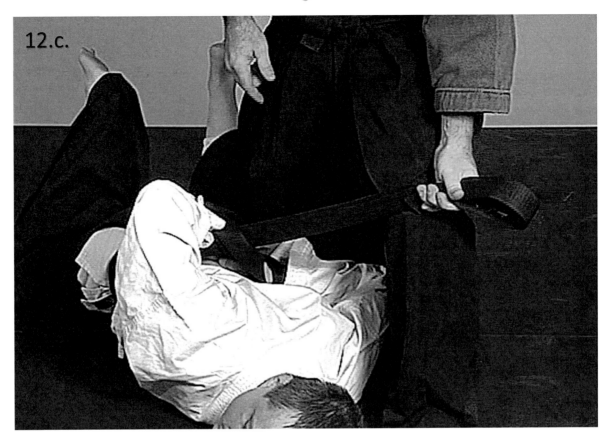

12.c. Once the Musubi has been tied and pulled through the defender can easily hold the assailant or subdue the attacker further or even strike with various attacks of their own.

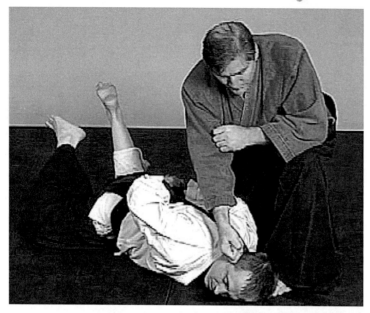

In this position the defender may strike or counter attack with variouse blows. Shuto (Knife Hand), Ken (Punch) or Ippon Ken (Knuckle strike)

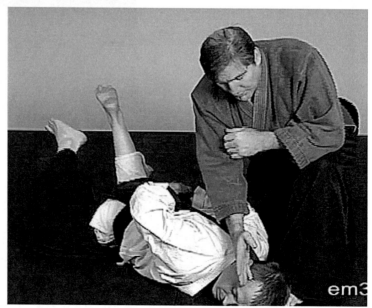

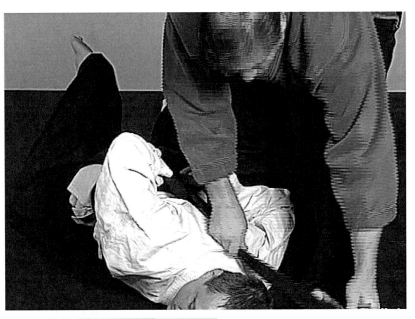

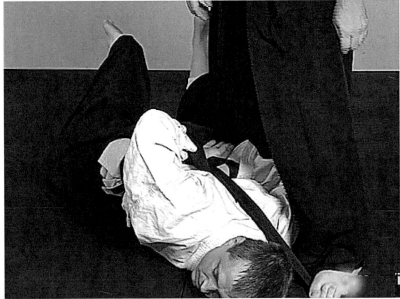

Once the rope is pulled the defender can use the foot to step on the rope or cord to keep the attacker subdued. This has the advantage of allowing the defender to utilize both hands to protect themselves or use the free hands to call for help.

Chapter 10

Revise the old for new

With the basic techniques represented in this manual the reader can have a better understanding of what traditional Hojojutsu is. From the art and history to the collective works of many. Using and understanding the techniques of Hojojutsu the art of binding is one of profound artistry.

As mentioned prior the art of Hojojutsu the Binding Art is one of contemporary movement and traditional theories. The noted foundations of this source is in its design and use. Since the earliest time periods of feudal samurai warriors the systemized use of the art of Hojojutsu which begun as a simplistic need for detainment has blossomed and grown in to an entire art form with in itself. One that encompasses more than simple sublimations and bindings but those masterful techniques that can be taught to defend oneself as well as subdue an attacker in various formations.

The history of Hojojutsu is varied and has been very obscure until recently. Japanese cultural history has complex and pervasive traditions of wrapping and tying in everyday life that go back for at least a millennium. These traditions touch on things as varied as Shinto votive items, the transportation & packing of foodstuffs, and Japanese traditional clothing which is tied to the body instead of being held with the buttons, pins and fasteners like that of western styled western dress. These factors have made any meaningful pinpointing of the historical origins of Hojojutsu problematic.

Japan's often violent history has made the mapping of meaningful changes in areas like armor and weaponry, including the studied use of rope for restraint as a technique that is Hojojutsu remains obscure. Nevertheless, the Hojojutsu techniques that have garnered attention in the last decade can be said to have flourished as a tool of law-enforcement under the Tokugawa Shogunate, and further on to current Law enforcement use as well.

With Japan divided into individual territories (Han) with the restrictions on travel already in place under Toyotomi Hideyoshi and strengthened afterwards by the successive Tokugawa reigns of the Edo period (1600-1868) provided a fertile ground for the development of formalized methods of tying prisoners who had to be transported across territories because of measures then in place mandating that a prisoner had to be handed off from one set of officials to another at the border of each territory with each law-enforcement group employing a different school's or region's often jealously-guarded methodology.

This spurred the growth in the importance of Hojojutsu and its use in the arrest of criminals and the codified methods of tying employed by various schools and agencies which sometimes provided numerous different methods of binding prisoners on the basis of considerations as different as social status, profession and sex of the prisoner with all of this added to the methods devised by those directly in the employ of the court system in Edo itself.

Techniques and methods

Generally speaking, Hojojutsu has been divided into two broad categories. The first is the capture and restraint of a prisoner that was effected with strong, thin cord (usually 3–4 millimeters) called a *hayanawa* or "fast rope", and sometimes the sageo carried by samurai on the sword-sheaths. In law-enforcement, this cord was carried by constables who secreted the rope in a small bundle that fed cord from one end. This *Torinawa* ("capture-rope") was coiled so that the cord would pay out from one end as the bundled cord was passed around the prisoner's body, neck and arms as he or she was tied. This was usually accomplished by one constable in the course of performing an arrest while the prisoner was actively resisting and had to be accomplished quickly.

Even at this stage, attention was still paid to visual and aesthetic concerns in the tying method as well as to the cultural needs of Japanese society. According to experts, an accused but not convicted prisoner would be tied using methods which allowed the prisoner to be securely restrained but which contained no knots to save the prisoner the shame of being publicly bound. Instead of securing the tie with knots, the constable held on to the free end of the rope and walked behind the prisoner to keep him or her under control as the prisoner was taken for an interrogation which could involve the application of one or more forms of judicial torture to elicit a confession.

The second category was effected with one or more "main ropes" or "Honnowa" which like the Torinawa could be any one of many different lengths, but was a proper hemp rope, possibly six or more millimeters in diameter and as much as eighty feet long which was used to provide a more secure, long-term binding than is possible with the Torinawa for transportation to a place of incarceration, restraint at legal proceedings, and in the case of particularly severe crimes for the public display of the prisoner prior to execution by such methods as beheading, crucifixion (i.e., the prisoner was displayed tied to a cross before spears were driven through the body), or, in arson convictions, death by fire.

Honnowa ties were applied by a group of people, usually not less than four, whose presence allowed the use of more intricate and ornate patterns than was the case with the Torinawa. Both forms combined effective restraint with a distinct visual aesthetic.

In either form, the Hojojutsu ties known today display a shrewd understanding of human anatomy through several recurrent themes. This can include leverage-removal (tying limbs in positions that decrease the force they can generate), rope-placement to discourage struggling or to make it less effective by placing one or more loops of rope around the neck and constricting restraint around points on the upper arms where determined struggle put pressure on blood vessels and nerves numbing the extremities.

Persistence in modern times

Hojojutsu shows limited survival in the modern world, both in Japan and elsewhere. Torinawa-techniques are taught as part of the curriculum learned by modern Japanese police officers and it remains an advanced topic within schools of jujutsu, following it and other Japanese traditional martial arts as they make their way around the world from Brazil to Eastern Europe.

Although the Honnawa techniques have long been supplanted by handcuffs and leg-irons, some teachers of traditional martial arts in Japan work to continue to maintain the art form. The Soke (head of, and heir to the style) of Masaki-ryu Bujutsu, Nawa Yumio, has written several books on the subject and has worked as an historical consultant on matters dealing with law-enforcement and Mizukoshi Hiro's recently reprinted book *Torinawajutsu* offers historical background followed by thorough, practical instruction in more than 25 traditional ties including some recreated from rare and very old texts. The Koryu cited are Seigo Ryu Jujutsu, Seishin Ryu Jujutsu, Koden Enshin Ryu Iaijutsu, Nanbu Handen Hojo Jutsu, Kurokawa Ryu Ninjutsu, Kurama Yoshin Ryu Jujutsu, Mitsuo (Mippa) Muteki Ryu, Bo Ryu and Tenfu Muso Ryu. Although long out-of-print, the late Seiko Fujita's monumental work, *Zukai Torinawajutsu* could be considered a bible of the art; showing hundreds of ties from many different schools.

Back to now

As I have stated clearly several times with in this manual I am not the preeminent authority in all things Hojojutsu related.

I would never want to feel I left anyone with that impression. It is my sincere hope that what lies with in this text is a helpful and reliable source of information to teach others a formidable and practical martial art and one that should be considered as a legitimate art form with conceivable and practical use in today's society.

As I travel the world and teach classes and seminars to the masses, I often reflect upon the traditions and value that I pass on.

My only goal in sharing the information in this manual is to promote and hold an undated art form to an entire new audience and renewal in to today's martial society.

With so many new arts available today in the word, it is often the best time of reflection to look back to where we once came from to find the roots of what we know to be true.

The Hojojutsu art and the art of binding is not in itself a complete or separate system. However, with that said it is important to note that the techniques that have been derived and passed down from teacher to student can be shared with other styles and arts.

The techniques of Hojojutsu and the art of binding is relevant today as it was 400 years prior. Although I do not teach specific strikes or patterns of defense, it is a viable art that can be easily incorporated in to any other art form that is taught today. Thus, anyone with training in this art or style of technique with the rope or cord can be used by or within many other styles to build on existing techniques and to learn the art of tying your enemy.

As with any other technique it can be applied to other martial arts and you too can share in the knowledge of Hojojutsu the binding art.

"Fighting isn't all there is to the Art of War. The men who think that way, and are satisfied to have food to eat and a place to sleep, are mere vagabonds.

A serious student is much more concerned with training his mind and disciplining his spirit than with developing martial skills."
—Miyomoto, <u>Musashi</u>

Chapter 11

About the Author

Shihan Allen Woodman has been studying martial arts since he was a child As a young man he discovered the world of martial arts early on while growing up on a military base outside Tokyo, Japan.

Woodman had studied the traditional Martial art of Shotokan Karate directly with Shihan Sensei Ryuichi Sato.

Sato, a direct student of O'Sensei Gichin Funakoshi for more than 15 years. Mr. Woodman received the Honorary title of Renshi Sensei 4th Degree Black Belt and master instructor from Sensei Makoto Nakamura, Sensei Sato's Top student in 1989. Training with his initial instructor Shihan Sato, he eventually earned his rank of 6th degree black belt at the Hombu in Japan.

Where most people would be content, Shihan Allen has devoted his life to learning and promoting martial arts as a whole. Arranging and performing martial arts demonstrations, events and classes for the Texas state Library system in the 1980's, California School District, and Instructor to the Bakersfield and Los Angeles Police department in the 1990's.

Shihan Allen Woodman has not only devoted his entire life to martial arts, with over 40 years plus in training and more than half of that in Asia. He is one of the most sought after instructors around today and has accumulated high levels of mastery and certified rank in many different arts.

Shihan Woodman has written over 32 books and co-authored many more with such great masters and teachers such as Soke Joe Miller, Nidai Soke Micheal DePasquale Jr., Master Cary Hiroyuki Tagawa, and Grandmaster Ramiro Estalilla.

Allen has devoted his life to martial arts training and learning. Also holding Dan ranks in Aikido and Jujitsu as well as earning instructor certification in Kabaroan Eskrima directly from Grandmaster Estalilla and training directly with Bruce Lee's teacher and Grandmaster of the Wing Chun system master Yip Chun in Hong Kong.

Todd. Sensei Todd himself was the first Foreign Student to ever receive a Black belt in Japan directly from Funakoshi Osensei in the late 1940s.

In 1994, Allen got another rare opportunity to train and study the art of Wing Chun Kung Fu with the Grandmaster Yip Chun, Son of Yip Man and teacher to Bruce Lee. His training continues to this day and brings a new side to his martial arts experience. He helped to bring Grandmaster Yip Chun and his top student Sifu Sam Kwok to the USA for an extensive tour, for the first time ever in American martial arts history in 1994.

During the early 1990s Sensei Allen became the personal and private student and Uchi Deshi of Shihan Sensei Walter

In 1988 he was introduced by longtime friend Ted LucayLucay to the Grandmaster of Eskrima Ramiro Estalilla. He continued training with him until receiving a 6th level Masters Instructors Certificate from the Grandmaster himself. Mr. Woodman has also trained extensively with other Filipino Grandmaster such as Dan Inosanto, Richard Bustillo, Cacoy Canete, Leo Giron, Angel Cabales, Narrie Babao and may others.

Never resting in his search for more in depth understanding of martial arts he was introduced to the great Sosai Mas Oyama and trained directly off and on with him over a two year period just before Oyamas death in 1994. Allen Woodman published the last known interview with the great master Oyama just prior to his death. For his efforts to help promote martial arts, Allen Woodman was inducted in to the World martial Arts hall of Fame in 1996, as Journalist of the Year.

Mr. Woodman has always been involved in sharing his knowledge with others and has done so at every avenue.

Mr. Woodman began publishing the regional martial arts magazine SIDEKICK from 1993-1998. Covering stories from traditional Karate, Aikido schools and Filipino Eskrima Arts but Indonesian and even Bando arts as well. Recently he re-launched the publication as a free digitally downloadable online magazine.

Throughout his career he has always sought out quality instructors and through his good friend Hanshi Otto Johnson another great Wado practitioner he was introduced to Shihan Joe Miller and the Taizan ryu Taiho Jutsu (Police Apprehension Program). After years of study with the founder of the art he eventually earned his Yudansha in that art form. Over a few years Allen and Joe became friends and Allen Co-Authored the first printed book on the Taizan Ryu

Taiho Jutsu system and subsequently produced a full instructional DVD together as well.

Eventually reuniting and training directly with Hanshi Otto Johnson in Wado Ryu, Sensei Woodman was asked to become the technical co-ordinator for the American Wado-Ryu Renmei by Mr. Johnson in 1995. As a longtime friend and martial arts colleague of Sensei Otto, they sat down together and had written out many ideas for the manual of the Wado ryu Federation, "Introduction to American Wado Ryu".

From 1994 - 1997 Allen promoted and held the Masters in Action events. These were the first and largest martial arts gatherings in the country at the time. Hosting over 60 martial arts masters at one time, teaching free and informative seminars to anyone in attendance. There were also martial arts and action movie stars on hand, to sign autographs and shake hands to adoring fans of all ages. In 1997 it was the staging ground for the

first ever Martial Arts Film Makers Awards (Crystal Awards).

In 1998 Allen returned to his roots and returned to training in Japan. He lived and trained in Tokyo, Japan and studied at the head schools of Aikido and Karate for the next 13 years before returning to the United States.

In 2011, Shihan Woodman returned to the U.S. to an outpouring of support and welcoming arms of students and teachers that wanted to share in the knowledge that Mr. Woodman has been the recipient of.

Shihan Allen Woodman has been inducted in over 10 Martial Arts Hall of Fames including 2X at Cynthia Rothrock's

Legends of Martial Arts Event, Alan Goldberg"s Action Magazine Hall of Honors Awards, 2X at the World Martial Arts Hall of Fame hosted by Dr. Enrico Moore, 4X by the USA Martial Arts Hall of Fame, 2X at World Karate Union Hall of Fame and honored at the prestigious World Sokeship Council, promoting him as one of the highest authorities on traditional martial arts. Recently Allen was also honored by the Martial Arts History Museum in 2013 and 2014 as a member of the Museum and for his many contributions to the martial arts community.

Shihan Allen Woodman Certifications and current Ranks

- 6th Dan   Traditional Karate Do Shotokan from the Hombu Dojo Japan   2010
- 6th Dan   Traditional Aikido at the Hombu Dojo, Japan   2009
- 6th Degree Guro / Master Kabaroan Eskrima Certification from GM Ramiro Estalilla. 2011
- 4th Dan Wado Ryu Karate Do certified by Hanshi Otto Johnson and Shihan Walter Todd.   1996
- 2nd Dan in Daito Ryu Jujitsu Under John Denora Sensei   1995
- 1st Dan Yudansha ranking in Taizan Ryu from Soke Joe Miller   2011
- 1st Dan Judo Certified Shihan Walter Todd   1990
- Certified Training Muay Thai. Coach Pakdi Pomprasong in Chang Mai, Thailand   1984
- Certified Training Kyokushin Karate Osensei Mas Oyama 1993
- Certified Training Wing Chun Grandmaster Yip Chun.   1994

Allen Woodman has spent over 25 years living and traveling throughout Asia learning from some of the greatest masters in martial arts history.

- Sensei Woodman has trained with Shihan Ryuechi Sato (Direct Student of Osensei Gichin Funakoshi, Founder of Shotokan Karate)
- Trained directly with Yip Chun, son of the late Great Grand Master of Wing Chun Yip Man and teacher to Bruce Lee.
- He has trained with the Late Founder of Kyokushin Karate Sosai Mas Oyama
- Studied at the Hombu Dojo in Japan for many years under the Doshou Ueshiba,
- Trained with Grandmaster Ramiro Estalilla Jr. in Kabaroan Eskrima
- Trained with Guro Ted LucayLucay in Temujin JKD /Kali
- Trained directly with Grandmaster Leo Giron in the Largo Mano system
- Trained Directly with Nidai Soke R. Okuyama in Hakko Ryu Jujitsu System

Allen Woodman's Personal Accomplishments

- Gold medal winner Texas Karate Tournament 1987
- Gold Medal winner Texas open Karate Championships 1988
- Grand champion Golden State Championships 1991
- Grand champion Magic Martial Arts Tournament 1992
- 1st place Weapons forms West coast Championships 1992
- New York State Full Contact Stick Fighting Champion 1997
- Contemporary Goju championships Champion1994

- Shihan Sensei Allen Woodman is a 10X times Inductee to the Martial Arts Hall of Fame. World Martial Arts Hall of fame, Universal Martial Arts Hall of Fame, World Karate Union Hall of Fame Legends of Martial Arts Hall of Fame and Gary Alexanders Hall of Fame I.A.M.A.

Magazines and Newspapers
(Mentioned/Articles)

- Rochester Gazzette Newspaper featured Article 1994
- SideKick magazine - SPECIAL MASTERS EDITION 1995
- SideKick Magazine Featured Article 1996
- Hindustani Times (INDIA) Cover story 2010
- Black Belt Magazine 1996
- Inderastan Newspaper (INDIA) Featured article 2010
- Intelligencer Featured article 2011
- Ephrata Review article 2012
- Hanford Times Article 1995
- Lemoore Eagle Article 1991
- Martial Pulse Featured Article 2012
- Action Magazine Featured Article 2012-2013
- Martial Science Magazine 2014
- Ciencia Marcial Magazine 2014

With all this history and experience, Shihan Allen Woodman has a singular mind set to teach and forward his knowledge and learning to others. Building community through communication is his motto and he lives what he teaches as a real Budo Ka for the 21st century.

"Real Budo in motion"

Cary Hiroyuki Tagawa

"A Great martial artist"

Cynthia Rothrock

"A benefit to martial arts everywhere"

Michael Matsuda

"A true student of the arts"

Dan Inosanto

"One of the best traditional artist"

Joe Miller

"A true Martial Arts Historian."

Michael DePasquale Jr.

"A Wealth of information"

Mark V. Wiley

"A real martial Artist, Great human being to know"

Eric Lee

"A benefit to martial arts everywhere"

Michael Matsuda

"Noteworthy instructor"

Richard Norton

"A martial artist in every sense."

Daniel Vena

"Sound instructor with knowledge"

Sam Kwok

"A real go getter"

Alan Goldberg

Shihan Allen Woodman is available for seminars and lectures. Please feel free to contact at any time.

senseiallenwoodman@yahoo.com

619 823 8819

GET YOUR COPY TODAY

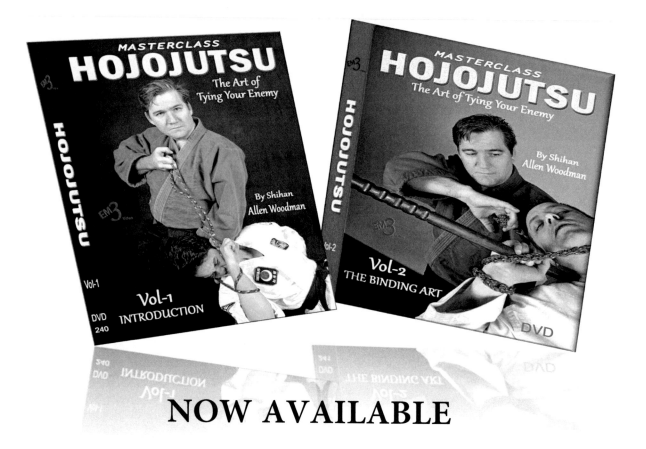

NOW AVAILABLE

HOJOJUTSU INSTRUCTIONAL DVD

DVD VOL. 1

In DVD one you will learn the basic moves and individual techniques of the fast rope and capture techniques used in the system. Taught by Shihan Allen Woodman Run time 39 minutes

$19.95

DVD VOL. 2

In DVD Two you will learn the more advanced techniques and moves of the fast rope and capture techniques used in the system. Including self-defense from the ground as well as Law Enforcement uses Taught by Shihan Allen Woodman Run time 58 minutes.

$29.95

Made in the USA
Middletown, DE
27 December 2015